Voyage into Space

HALF and HALF

GREAT STORY & COOL FACTS

Introduction

Welcome to Half and Half books, a great combination of story and facts! You might want to read this book on your own. However, the section with real facts is a little more difficult to read than the story. You might find it helpful to read the facts section with your parent, or someone else, who can help you with the more difficult words. Your parent may also be able to answer any questions you have about the facts—or at least help you find more information!

Voyage into Space

English Edition Copyright © 2008 by Treasure Bay, Inc.
English Edition translated by Elizabeth Bell and edited by Sindy McKay

Original edition Copyright © Éditions Nathan (Paris, France), 2000
Original Edition: Voyager dans l'espace

My Birthday on the Moon by Hubert Ben Kemoun
Illustrated by Colonel Moutarde

Non-fiction text by Christian Grenier
Non-fiction illustrations and vignettes: Matthieu Blanchin, Gwen
Activity by Anita Camier and Marie le Doze

Photography Credits:
PhotoDisc, NASA, ESA and archives Nathan

Special thanks to Christèle Frinzine

Special thanks to NASA, as well as Carla Rosenberg, Katherine Trinidad
and Ruth Netting for their assistance on this book.

Published by Treasure Bay, Inc.
40 Sir Francis Drake Boulevard
San Anselmo, CA 94960 USA

PRINTED IN SINGAPORE

Library of Congress Catalog Card Number: 2008922566

Hardcover ISBN-13: 978-1-60115-209-1
Paperback ISBN-13: 978-1-60115-210-7

Visit us online at:
www.HalfAndHalfBooks.com

Voyage into Space

Table of Contents

Story: My Birthday on the Moon

Facts: Space Travel

My Birthday on the Moon

Story by **Hubert Ben Kemoun**
Illustrated by **Colonel Moutarde**

1

Oh no! I won!

"No, no, no, no, no! I don't want to go!"

"But you won the lottery, Naram," said my father. He pointed to the mail message his computer was projecting onto the living room wall. "Out of all the children born on July 20th, 2069, you were chosen to go to the moon!"

"It's not my fault I was born on July 20th," I pouted. "They should just pick someone else."

Mom gave me a stern look. "You're being silly, Naram. This is a wonderful opportunity. I wish your father and I were going to the moon!"

"I wish you were, too," I muttered under my breath.

Now it was my father's turn to give me a stern look.

"There's nothing to do on the moon, Dad," I protested. "And they want me to stay there for one whole week. I'll miss my own birthday party!"

"This experience will be much more exciting than a birthday party." He pointed again to the message on the wall. "Just look at all the things you get to do!"

NARAM

You are the lucky winner of a dream week
in the beautiful lunar city of Luna 3000!

You will stay at the Meteor,
a five-comet luxury hotel.

Your room will have a dazzling view
of the setting Earth.

For your entertainment, we have planned
a space-cycle trip across the Sea of Tranquility,
plus two days at Luna Park
with free admission to all the rides.

Rounding out this spectacular week
will be a huge party at the Luna 3000 palace
with the Governor of the moon.

"You'll be traveling first class," added my mother enthusiastically. "Doesn't that sound wonderful?"

"No! It sounds awful," I yelled as I ran to my bedroom.

I threw myself on my bed and stared up at the ceiling. I felt badly about the way I had reacted to the news of my trip to the moon. It really was kind of exciting. I just wished it wasn't happening on my birthday!

My computer telephone rang. I answered and the face of my good friend, Dolly, appeared on the screen.

"Hi, Naram," she said. "What's new?"

"Disaster!" I replied. "They held a lottery for everyone born on July 20th, 2069 and my name was picked. I'm going to the moon—on my birthday!"

"*On your birthday?*" she repeated in shock. "Why?"

"July 20, 2079 will be exactly 110 years after the first human set foot on the moon. There's going to be a big celebration and I have to be the guest of honor!"

"But what about your party?" asked Dolly in dismay.

Finally, someone understood why I was so upset!

2

Save My Party!

How could my parents do this to me? They knew I had been planning a very special 10th birthday party since the day after my 9th birthday. I had bargained with them for months to let me take my three best friends to Tahitium.

Tahitium is an orbital space station, hovering above the Pacific Ocean. It has about one hundred time-share units, and my parents' unit has two small bedrooms, a kitchen, a bathroom, and a living room looking out on the Polynesian islands, west of Australia.

Going there by orbital bus with my best friends would be much more fun than taking a luxury spaceship to the moon all by myself. And spending two whole days with them was much more important to me than celebrating the first step ever taken on the moon.

The news about my winning the lottery spread at supersonic speed. My name and face were seen all over the planetary circuit. You'd think I had discovered a uranium mine on Pluto or something!

In my History of the Galaxy class, the teacher asked me what I knew about Neil Armstrong, the man who had taken that first step on the moon. I guess I was supposed to be an expert because he had taken the step on the same date as my birthday. But all I knew was that I was born on July 20th, 2069 and his trip to the moon was on July 20th, 1969.

The teacher showed the class some blurry, old-fashioned film of the 1969 moon landing. The class laughed as they watched astronauts Armstrong and Aldrin walking clumsily across the surface of the moon in their big, bulky spacesuits.

We also watched an old film of the very first man in space, Yuri Gagarin. It was hilarious! The windows of his orbiter—not even a shuttle!—were ridiculously small next to the huge bay windows of our modern spacecrafts. Gagarin could barely move in his tiny capsule, while we can walk around, shop, or go to the movies in our shuttles.

It was all pretty funny, but I didn't join in the laughter. All I could think about was the birthday trip

that I was going to miss. Lisbeth, Cindy, Dolly, and I had planned on having so much fun going down to the island beaches, just four miles below Tahitium. We were even going to pack our own picnic lunch— spaghetti noodle sandwiches and sour apple chips.

I was feeling so sorry for myself that I went straight home after school. Waiting for me there was Ms. Marie, the organizer of the Luna 3000 festivities.

"Naram, you must be so excited about your visit to the moon!" she beamed. "What an amazing way to spend your birthday!"

I suddenly realized that she was right. It probably would be amazing. "Thank you," I said. "I just wish my friends could come with me."

She gave me an understanding smile. "It is nice to share a memorable experience with good friends. Unfortunately, we don't have a good reason to send them with you. It wouldn't be fair to the other children born on July 20th who had hoped to be the lucky one!"

"What if there was a good reason—could they come then?" I asked.

"Well, I suppose they could," Ms. Marie replied with a surprised grin.

My face lit up with hope. "Really?"

Ms. Marie nodded. "But it would have to be a very, very good reason."

My brows furrowed in thought as an idea began to take shape in my head . . .

3

Luna 3000

I guess my idea was a pretty good one, because soon the four of us were on our way, traveling first class to Luna 3000!

"I hope this works, Naram," said Dolly.

"It's worked so far, hasn't it?" I replied.

"Well, even if it doesn't totally work, this traveling part is really fun!" said Cindy.

I again assured my friends that everything was going to be fine. After all, we had all studied very hard. We now probably knew more about the history of space exploration than the people who had actually been there!

Just then, Ms. Marie appeared in the doorway of our shuttle cabin. She had a no-nonsense look on her face as she gave us a few last words of advice:

"The media and several local officials will be there when you step off the shuttle, girls. They'll be asking lots of questions, so be prepared!"

The four of us looked at each other and grinned.

"Don't worry, Ms. Marie," Lisbeth reassured her. "We know all about the era of space pioneers. After all, some of those people were our ancestors!"

"Hmm . . . So you've said," replied Ms. Marie with a twinkle in her eye.

I wasn't quite sure what Ms. Marie meant by that, but there was no time to worry about it now. Our shuttle was landing! The pilot brought us down smoothly on the main runway of Luna 3000. We all got butterflies in our stomachs when we looked out the window and saw the huge crowd that had gathered.

A band played in our honor as we moved down the long walkway to the·main shuttle-port.

Ms. Marie spoke to the reporters first:

"Ladies and gentlemen, I would like to introduce the four girls who have been selected to spend this exceptional week on Luna 3000. Three of the girls are descendants of very important members of the early space programs. And Naram, our guest of honor, was born on July 20th, 2069! That's exactly 100 years after that historic space walk. Enjoy your chat with them!"

We were sensational! My friends told the reporters everything they knew about their astronaut "ancestors."

Dolly and Lisbeth talked about being descendants of Neil Armstrong and Edwin "Buzz" Aldrin, the astronauts who had first walked on the moon in July 1969.

Cindy spoke of her great-great uncle, Yuri Gagarin, the first human in space.

No one would have ever guessed that my friends weren't really related to these

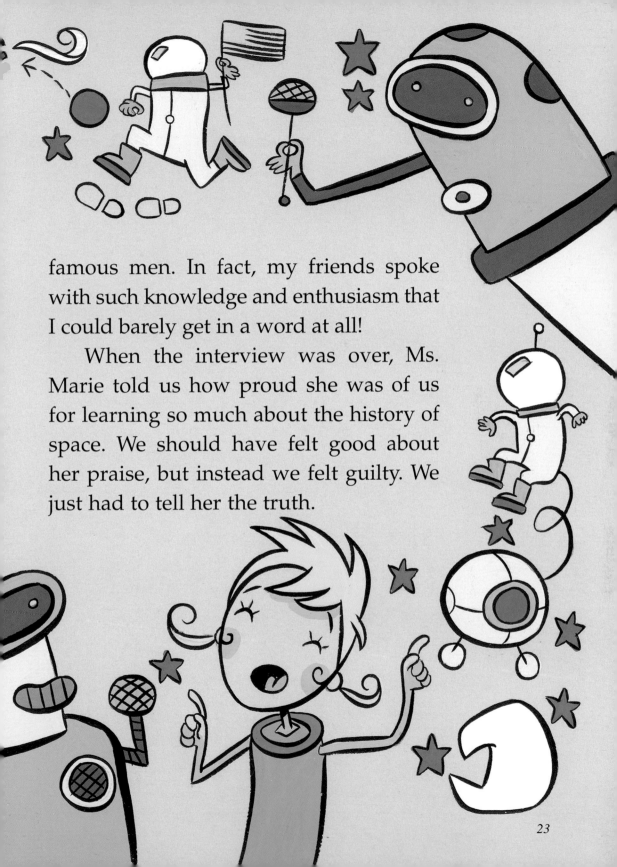

famous men. In fact, my friends spoke with such knowledge and enthusiasm that I could barely get in a word at all!

When the interview was over, Ms. Marie told us how proud she was of us for learning so much about the history of space. We should have felt good about her praise, but instead we felt guilty. We just had to tell her the truth.

"My friends don't really have ancestors who were in the early space programs," I confessed. Ms. Marie raised her eyebrows in surprise as I continued, "We just made that up so you would let them come here with me."

"I'm afraid you're wrong," replied Ms. Marie.

Now it was our turn to be surprised.

"I thought you might try a little trick like this, so I did some research. It turns out your friends really are related to people who worked in the early space programs. You are as well, Naram! Not the famous astronauts you talked about today. But all of you have an ancestor that helped put those famous astronauts into space. You might want to do a little research on your great-grandparents and see what you discover!"

We all eagerly agreed to do just that as soon as we got home. But right now, it was time to hop on our space-cycles and head for the Black Hole roller coaster at Luna Park!

Surviving In Space

On Earth, we walk and breathe without even thinking about it. In space, those things are not so easy! There is no up or down, and we are weightless. That makes it hard to walk. Space is a vacuum, with no air, so breathing without proper equipment is impossible.

"The dream is alive"

Astronaut John W. Young
—first Space Shuttle mission

The Earth is surrounded by a protective layer of gases we call the atmosphere. The atmosphere shields us from dangerous cosmic rays and too much sunlight. It also regulates the weather. Above the atmosphere, temperatures are 248°F facing the sun . . . and -298°F on the shady side.

"That's one small step for man,
one giant leap for mankind."

Neil Armstrong's first step on the moon,
July 20th, 1969

Survival in space is only possible in special man-made environments, such as shuttles, space stations, or individual space suits. Even within these environments, weightlessness is still a problem. Since an astronaut is always floating and never bearing weight, his or her muscles soon begin to weaken from lack of use.

Intensive Training

It takes hard work!
Becoming an astronaut takes hard work and determination. Astronauts undergo a long training program on Earth to prepare them to live for days, weeks and sometimes even months in space. Many people would like to become astronauts, but only a few are chosen for the training programs. Some people apply several times before they are chosen.

Many try but **few are chosen.**

Who are the astronauts?
They are scientists, mathematicians, engineers, doctors, biologists, pilots— the list goes on and on! Candidates for training are chosen based on their experience, potential, motivation, teamwork skills, communication skills, adaptability and love of learning. They also must be in good physical condition. Training lasts two to three years.

Training in a swimming pool . . .
Astronauts go underwater in a huge pool to train for space walks. The pool is called the Neutral Buoyancy Lab. This huge tank is forty feet deep!

Training in a plane . . .
True conditions of weightlessness exist in an airplane that is plunging straight down in a nosedive. Everything starts floating inside the fuselage, just as in an orbiting spacecraft. But this can only last 20 seconds . . . because the airplane must quickly right itself!

Learning to survive . . .
When the space capsule returns to Earth it may land far from the intended site. Since they might land in the remote wilderness, and it might take awhile to pick them up, astronauts must know how to build a shelter, how to fish, and how to hunt.

The Long Journey

Astronauts are guinea pigs!
Doctors and biologists study the human body in space. Strange things happen to the body due to weightlessness. Blood rises to the head, bones become brittle, and hearing and sleep are altered. To reach Mars, people would have to live in space for months. Scientists hope to find a way to withstand the journey.

Animals and plants in space . . .
To live for months in space, astronauts will have to grow their own food. That's one reason so many food experiments are conducted on space flights. For example, scientists may observe how an egg hatches. Or, they may observe how a grain of wheat sprouts, grows, and orients itself in orbit, where there is no "up"! Scientists also conduct experiments in hopes of creating new medicines and vaccines.

Astronauts are space mechanics.
They may replace electric batteries, repair a telescope, or attach solar panels . . . But these are delicate operations. Using a hammer in conditions of weightlessness drives the hammer up and away from the object being struck! And, if you use a screwdriver without being strapped down, your body will turn instead of the screw!

To leave the space station, astronauts must wear space suits that provide oxygen and heat. Going outside is dangerous and difficult. It is always done in pairs. Both astronauts are attached to the space station with long straps. Tools must also be attached with cords or straps, so they don't float away if they're dropped!

A Day in the Life of an Astronaut

Watch out for floating crumbs!
Food on a space mission comes prepackaged. The food can be heated in a forced air convection oven. Drinking in space always requires a straw. An astronaut must drink 3 liters of water per day to avoid dehydration.

Two hours of exercise per day.
In space, muscles grow smaller and weaker. Astronauts keep fit with a treadmill, a stationary bike, and a rowing machine.

Sleeping in space.
Some astronauts sleep in individual sleeping compartments. Some simply secure their sleeping bags to the floor, ceiling, or wall. Many wear eye masks to shield their eyes from the light. They may also use earplugs to block out the sound of loud instruments and radio communication in the cabin.

Personal hygiene.
Astronauts take "sponge baths" in space, using wet towels. There are also toilets in space. A specially designed toilet called a Waste Collection System (WCS) collects and stores the waste so it can be brought back to Earth for safe disposal.

Time off.
Crew members listen to the radio, watch videos, and communicate with their families. They also observe the Earth. From 200 miles up, they can see the contours of rivers and the routes of highways.

Rockets and Starships

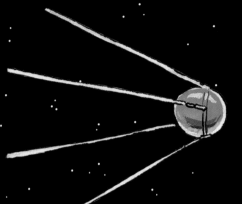

On October 4, 1957, Russia launched the first manmade satellite, Sputnik I. A month later, the Russians sent a dog named Laika into space. And on April 12, 1961, they sent up the first human being, Yuri Gagarin. All of this inspired the United States to try to beat the Russians to the moon with Project Apollo.

A launch rocket's life span is less than 10 minutes... A satellite can last several centuries!

The dream of placing a human being on the moon became a reality in July, 1969. After a 3-day journey, three Apollo astronauts went into orbit around the moon. On July 20th, astronauts Neil Armstrong and Edwin "Buzz" Aldrin left the command ship in a lunar module. They landed on the moon and stayed there for 21 hours.

In December, 1972, Apollo 17 astronauts tested the first moon rover vehicle on the surface of the moon. This allowed them to travel for several miles without effort.

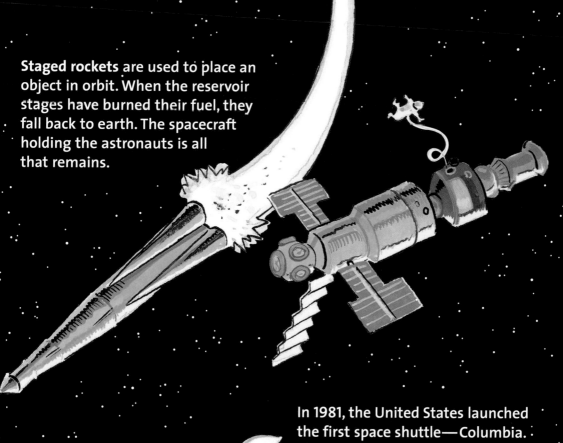

Staged rockets are used to place an object in orbit. When the reservoir stages have burned their fuel, they fall back to earth. The spacecraft holding the astronauts is all that remains.

In 1981, the United States launched the first space shuttle—Columbia. Shuttles are launched with a rocket, but land like an airplane upon returning to Earth. In the central portion of a shuttle is a space lab where the astronauts do their work. In 1986, the Soviets built what was practically a house in space: the MIR space station. For 15 years, the station hosted different teams of scientists.

Construction on the **International Space Station** began in 1998 and has since replaced MIR as an important base for scientific studies in space. Many countries are working together to build the International Space Station.

Living on the Moon?

During the 21st century, humans might build a **permanent habitable space station on the moon**. Several projects are now being considered. This small city would probably consist of different domed areas linked to each other. Certain lodgings might be built underground for protection against meteorites and solar rays.

An Earth colony on the moon! Someday scientists may live on the moon where they can study the lunar rocks and subsoil. They might install powerful telescopes on the moon's surface to study the universe unhampered by the atmosphere and pollution on Earth.

A lunar transport?
On the moon, gravity is 6 times weaker than on Earth. That makes takeoff a lot easier! This is why the moon could someday become an astro-port for Earth. Spaceships traveling to distant planets could take off and land there.

A weekend on the moon—just a dream?

For a long time, moon travel will be reserved for astronauts and scientists. Even the very rich will probably not be able to vacation there in the 21st century!

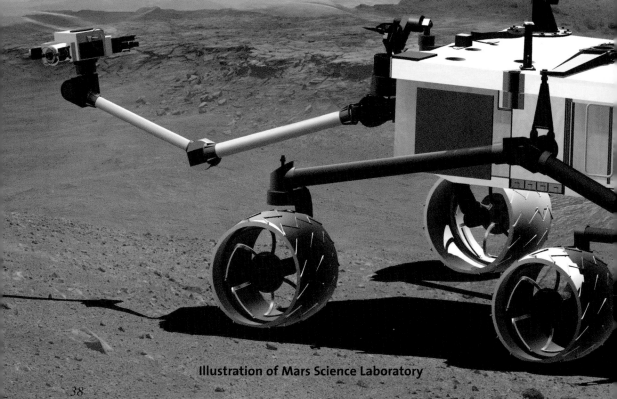

Mars...and beyond

Will we travel to the stars someday?

Mars is the planet in our solar system that is most similar to Earth. It has polar ice caps and clouds in its atmosphere. It has seasonal weather patterns, soil, volcanoes, and canyons. Its temperature ranges from from 68°F to -220°F. Several robotic probes have already been sent there.

A two year journey!
When Mars is closest to the Earth, it is still more than 150 times the distance from the Earth to the moon. To get to Mars we will need a space vehicle in which astronauts could grow their own food and recycle water. The crew would have to deal with isolation, unexpected illness, and the effects of weightlessness and cosmic rays.

Illustration of Mars Science Laboratory

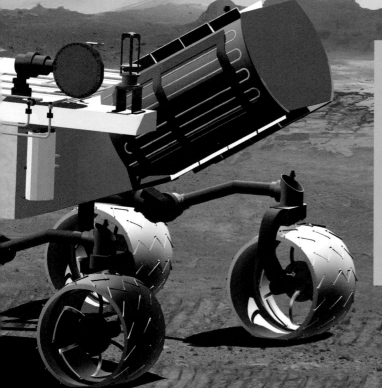

Exploring Mars

In 2004, two robotic "rovers" landed on Mars after a long journey from Earth. These rovers were designed to collect information about Mars. They could rove about 100 yards across the surface of Mars each day. A new robotic rover, known as the Mars Science Laboratory, is planned to land on Mars in 2010. It will collect Martian soil and rock samples and analyze them to see if Mars could support any form of life, either now or in the past.

Message for extraterrestrials!

Two spacecraft, known as Voyager 1 and Voyager 2, were launched in 1977 to explore our solar system. They were originally designed to last for five years and visit two planets. However, they have far exceeded expectations. The Voyagers have explored all the giant outer planets of our solar system, as well as 48 of their moons. Both of these spacecraft are now continuing their journey beyond the solar system into interstellar space. Voyager 2 carries a large gold-plated CD that contains all kinds of information about the Earth and human life. Maybe someday it will be found by extraterrestrials who will try to decode all the information!

Other habitable planets may exist somewhere. If they do exist, they orbit other suns very far away. Unfortunately, even if we could design a space ship that could fly to another solar system, it would probably take many thousands of years for the space ship to fly there.

Liftoff!

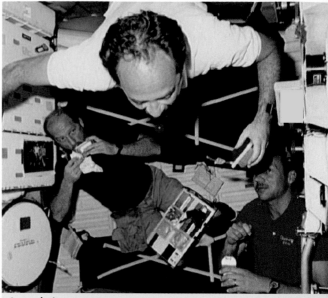

Lunch in space

Astronauts

A handyman in space

Room with a view of Earth

Astronauts must drink using a straw

Two hours of exercise a day

in Space

Out of the space station and into space!

An astronaut must get two hours of exercise each day to avoid muscle loss.

True

The journey of a rocket launching an astronaut into orbit lasts less than 10 minutes.

True

Did You Know?

How much would the International Space Station weigh on Earth?

   a. About 150,000 lbs.
   b. About 500,000 lbs.
   c. About 1,000,000 lbs.

c. About 1,000,000 pounds.

An astronaut, who is weightless in space, is taller than on the Earth.

True

Astronauts never take off without a passport and many visas.

True. They may make an emergency landing anywhere on Earth

From 1961 to 2000, how many human beings traveled in space?

30?
300?
3,000?

1961   2000

300

In 1984, Challenger carried into space several thousand:

a. Bees?
b. Earthworms?
c. Cockroaches?

a. Challenger carried several thousand bees to study their behavior under weightlessness.

The Hubble space telescope is as big as:

a. A box of laundry soap?
b. A bus
c. The Eiffel Tower

b. Launched into orbit in 1990, it is as big as a bus.

43

Your Satellite of Secrets

You can use this paper-mache satellite to hide small objects, your Christmas gift list, coded messages... Hang it on the ceiling of your room. Only you and the extraterrestrials will be able to reach it!

You will need:

Your parent's help and permission
2 round balloons
Newspaper torn into strips
Flour paste (flour mixed with a little water)
Silver paint
Straws
Nylon thread
Plastic bottle tops
Colored foam or cotton balls

1 Blow up the balloons and prepare the paste. Dip the newspaper strips in the paste and cover the balloons with at least 4 layers. Leave an opening around the neck of one of the balloons. Let dry for 2 days.

2 Pop the balloons with a pin. Cut in half the sphere without the opening. This is the lid of the satellite.

3 Make 4 X-shaped slits in the lid and slip the straws through from the inside. Attach the straws with paper-mache.

Cotton balls glued to the end of the straws.

4 Paint the satellite and lid with silver paint.

5 With a needle, make 2 small holes in the lid and in the satellite. Attach the cover with nylon thread knotted at each end, as shown.

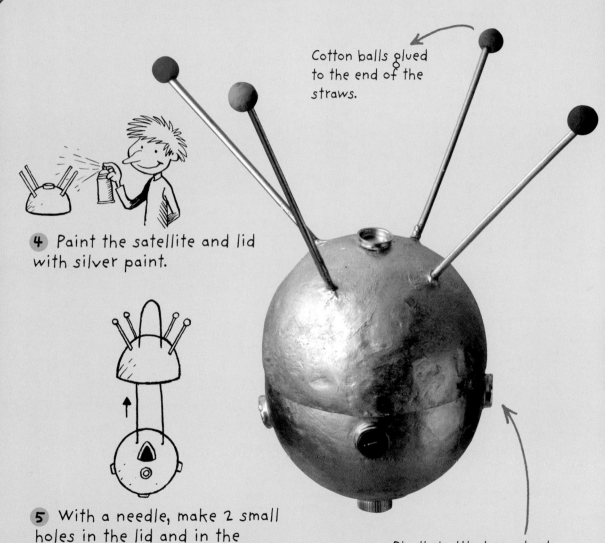

Plastic bottle tops glued to the box and lid

If you liked **Voyage into Space,** here is another
Half and Half™ book you are sure to enjoy!

Get a great story and cool facts about ancient Egypt!

In the story, a young girl wants to go with her father to see the building of the pyramids. Her father leaves without her, saying it is no place for a young girl. Then, she notices some-thing important he left behind. Facing dangers she did not expect, she sets out to find her father—and also see the creation of one of the greatest wonders of the world.

After the story, you can see for yourself how people lived long ago in this ancient land. Plus, find out more about the amazing pyramids they built—and how the mummies of their great Pharaoh kings were buried in those pyramids!

To see all the Half and Half books that are available,
just go online to **www.HalfAndHalf.com**